FINISHING LINE PRESS

www.finishinglinepress.com

Working Hypothesis

poems by

Charles Malone

Finishing Line Press
Georgetown, Kentucky

Working Hypothesis

ACKNOWLEDGMENTS

I have learned so much from so many—teachers and students—and I would
only fail in an attempt to offer complete thanks here. This book is much
indebted to Matthew Cooperman, Sasha Steensen, and Dan Beachy-Quick,
Felicia Zamora, Carrie George, Sony Ton-Aime, and Michael McLane. I owe
gratitude to Brittany Boord for her editorial help. The poets of Fort Collins,
Colorado and Kent, Ohio built communities that make this kind of work
possible. Thanks also to Susan Hazel Rich who has made a home where art
and poetry can grow.

I owe thanks to the editors and staff of the following journals where earlier
versions of some of these poems appear: "Beneficial Insects" *Toho Journal*,
"Beast Machines" *Ponder Review*, "About the River" *Montana Mouthful*, and
"Solstice" *Still: The Journal*.

Publisher: Leah Maines
Editor: Christen Kincaid
Cover Art: Aaron Foster *Catapult*
Author Photo: Caleb Young
Cover Design: Susan Hazel Rich

Order online: www.finishinglinepress.com
            also available on amazon.com

Author inquiries and mail orders:
Finishing Line Press
P. O. Box 1626
Georgetown, Kentucky 40324
U. S. A.

Table of Contents

"early morning, corrected poems, then anatomy of frogs"

—an example of a typical journal entry by Johann Wolfgang von Goethe from Andrea Wulf's *The Invention of Nature.*

I. DOMESTIC SCIENCE

Beneficial Insects

I want you to look at me the way
you look at the Eastern Dobsonfly—

like I could bite your finger right off
though I can't, or like I was once

a hellgrammite—an alien child,
like my biology has its own rules

which it does and we know this.
I want you to look at me with interest

when I lean in for a kiss in a cinematic
shaft of light under Breakneck Bridge

our wet bottoms on a mossy boulder
below the waterfall.

Downstream, a fisherman and his daughter
turn stones looking for bait

pure water clouds with their disturbances—
Don't look at me like I am a pure stream,

you say, *like I am hiding life
in my shadows.*

In Vivo

for my Mother

There is the lab
and there is the lab I imagine you working in—

those flasks and beakers
marked with milliliters, liquid bubbling, bleach aroma.

There is the lab that sells biological buffers, reagent biochemicals
in other words, purity and glow—

in other words, poetry
life fluoresces, enzymes produce and they change everything.

You make a chemical that reads the way I want to
and come home lit purple

an accidental spill,
by design living tissue activates a dye

alive, alive, alive each splotch asserting / reading
if there was an analog

a way to cover a stanza in an agent
that would show us which parts breathe.

Horace wrote about reading a man to death.
Here, the chemical opposite.

In death, the cell tissues ash
structures reduce to inky carbon

even illumination
ends.

Beast Machines

We stand awkwardly in our bodies
looking at the painting of the big lie.
While I am unable to find a figure,
she is certain there is man, but
our friend asks if it is a man or *the*—
We are all sure there is no woman
in the lie. She loves how sweet
and personal the painting is,
how it knows, and how she knows
it doesn't know, and that its sweetness
is a sugar-coating, robin's egg blue
and glued to animal skin and bone.

This is what we take in: A field
of white or black, clumped paint
thick like snow or soot or love
just a few points of color among gentle
marks of palette knives and a signature
carved back to the canvas, unreadable.
We forget, for the whole time that we
are looking at it, the whole time we
argue and interpret, we are wholly
alive, the hard floor pushes up through
our hips to remind us of this, to nudge us
to a room full of paintings of dead animals
from the Dutch school of the 17th century.
The frames have been treated with beeswax.
I cough and it echoes coldly through the gallery.

The Chemist's Son

Ours, the only house with a grid
of test-tubed tissue samples under a grow light,
Latinate names handwritten down their sides,
the tiniest leaves emerging in the basement.
Of course we are an experiment. "Let me show you,"
I would say to friends, descending.

Give the boy a toy that asks a question,
a microscope, a grow-your-own crystals kit—
without supervision, they were never as spectacular
as the image on the box. A side effect
of single-motherhood. This art,
shallower purple than natural amethyst.

In the kitchen, where we rarely eat, a pet painted turtle
with a lawnmower blade-shaped notch
in her shell. Carefully, we keep her whole.
A fridge shelf clatters with bottles of animal medicine.
I set fire to a table when I leave a magnifying glass
to record the bullfrogs with a tape deck, afternoon sun
lines up with accident like an ancient monolith.

She balances homework equations on a napkin
for the beautiful waitress at the diner —
a girl I am too shy to talk to.
Everywhere the apparati and texts
of inquiry and discovery, nothing more loved
than curiosity, yet she turns down the clinical trial.

Not everything is a science—the working hypothesis
is not always the most important.
The telescope's eyepiece has gone missing,
like the microscope's reflecting mirror.
Is there faith in how things turn out in absence?
The plants grow to the tops of their tubes
and choke. We never publish our results.

A Mild Earthquake

a flutter in the lungs and a laundry basket
quivers—your fingertip along the plastic basket's
cracked handhold, cotton, poly-blends, so dry
and smelling of lavender or Arm & Hammer
is it the refrigerator compressor? is it the earth?

we've always had problems with sequence, our steps
bipedal, shaky but every year a better mop, rattling,
tools have their own *Road to Homo Sapiens*, in the garage
I run a fingertip against steel threading—sharp, coated in black
grease, a rubberized hammer handle trembles on the bench

two glass vases kiss*tink* on a table built from an iron sewing base
we have problems understanding a longer view of time,
"The house has been here over a hundred years," or the
house was not here for 4.5 billion /
                                    / precipice clock, nervous
                    ticking ice age
                                    earthquake, your fingertip
against your lover's
elbow,
              shaking, spinning together
                            waiting to ask a question
that goes a gentle 4.2 on the scale.

Roots

is the schematic of kudzu or knob and tube

unkind to talk of one's kind one's rhizomatic thoughts

genetic fallacy—not all of us, but enough of us

have taken long sips of fermented stereotypes and live up

to the worst of white folks, creeping rootstalks

lit up like a Christmas tree on the Fourth of July

who lived on this street before, which houses were Iroquois

dried chicory root and coffee darker than the inside of a cow

ragged sailors with hearts like asters

ego's lineal functional psychosocial family

Dear Dad, the ditch is lined with wild bachelor's button

Post Hoc Ergo Propter Hoc

"You and your sister," my mother says
when I ask what she and my father
had in common
twenty years after the divorce.

She is a chemist
and she knows what she is doing,
leaving the equation unbalanced
letting the ions and radicals hunger
letting the charge hover
too tired to tidy up.

She is a chemist and knows
what odd numbers do to
protons and electrons
to stability, to the luminescence
of the sun, she knows how metals
grant gemstones their color

knows
how an answer is less valuable
than a question, how bonds are made
and broken, how history
is blood, how the rebellion
in her own cells
rips and scars and turns her
liver into her killer.

Weekly Weather Report

"Another word for father is worry." —*Li-Young Lee*

To love the man but not his memes
means multiplicity, open a box of names.
Love the the slack moment of cheek
before the anecdote that says he knows
better, but can't stop. Call it *momentum*.
Nonverbal as tremors leaving his writing
like an EKG or seismograph. Name this
tenderness.

Another word for love is *weather*. Each week
he looks up my forecast before calling to ask about it.
Never ask a question
you don't already know the answer to.
You can choose any number of words
for this advice. They say as much about you.

Another word might be *certainty*.
Certainty hands out candy to the kids,
chips in with the Chamber of Commerce
and the vintage car show. Certainty walks
the dog and shares all the news. Orders
blueberries in his pancakes,
because Certainty's doctor says they are good for him.
You or I can be jealous of the certainty
he moves through the world with
and still not be spiteful. At least one of us.

Another word for *son* is *weather*.
Moving over the landscape
of a life at an entirely different speed
at a distance, but still able
to scratch and hurt, to caress.

I rained today, father. I froze then I let the sap
of the forest run wild. I burnt everything with my seeing
then I dissipated.

Year Books

I remember you
just a 12-year-old white kid carving swastikas into paint
a metal bathroom stall
       trying to tick off hippie parents, then the
internet. I remember you pressing your palm
hard
       into the fold between muscles
of your own neck
closing carotid, turning purple
coming back gasping, laughing
now look at you,
           now look at you
your 12-year-old kid listening at the dinner table
thinking of ways,
       to trigger, to trouble, to make you proud
you with a small hammer popping master locks
popping pills, popping off
and all those bad ideas born in boredom
waiting,
       that double helix of hate
twisting and passing down.

Glue a Paper Globe

after Susanna Crum

dry lip each word
hurtled into community   hurt to sound, dawn
dawns unbelonging, "I have been thinking
about my soul" each word finding
balance of definition and history
separately   ear words and
mouth words
brain and bible words
science words and medical
measure or process
"I will come and see your new place
when I get better"
     better a measure
come to see process actively
end   you a chemist after all
"look what I have made for you"
I have *readied*
each blue sliver   paper point marquise
and now we have a globe
stinking with new mulch
each shredded yard each
workers start early
trucks idle   hands off tools
before our limbs hurtle material
into arrangement
labor into arrangement
each egg collection nestly each
house expressing
more than we intend

Great Little Fears

The world shrinks to the size of my vocabulary.
I go the same places and say the same things;
I hear the same people speaking.
The Dante translator says English is rhyme-poor
and he abandons terza rima for quatrains.
Reciprocity is a language.

The world shrinks to what's left after rent, to the range
of our gas tank—To the few hours before darkness
A limited number of interactions with a limited number
of characters. Community an umbrella stretched, run, ribbed.

The work shrinks to the ambition of my questions,
To the cleanliness of my hands;
The repetition of planting in a team.
Specialization thrives :

A concept like the flea or mosquito,
and the doctor repeats platitudes we've all heard
small-screen characters say.
Oncology is a small field of doctoring.
The liver has specific functions.

I don't know if nostalgia is a shrinking or a growing.
To expand the work to the scope of high school—
questions the shape of a period.
Sound clearly delineates.

The field of garlic bulbs frosts.
The growing onions are under snow.
We conduct a simple experiment
to measure acceleration by gravity;
we trigger a reaction that turns a penny silver by zinc.

Tender Engines

I write two words from a railway schematic, a serendipitous pairing. You ask what I am doing. You often ask if the poem is about you. I am never certain—how to answer my own aboutness? What's in the firebox? How many ways to stoke and steam 6 tons of words? Like rapture. But more spiritual than religious. More concentrated than blissful.

You are the space within which the poetry can exist. You are architecture :: an old house / a modest railway museum / a boiler :: The tender accompanies. It carries. Makes the work of the engine possible. We take turns fueling one another. We take turns burning the currency / stretching the world wide enough for the other / and others / so many to carry over the river.

The ferryman is a caring man. This river rises with rain. We are in question. Raptured questions. About the world. About the space it spins in. About the people spinning around in cars. Engines tuned and tended. My student says the first draft of this is an industrial love poem. Yet beyond us there is no offer of harmony —

Just water. Spinning. Just coal and steam. "The poem is just steam," I say, "a gentle vapor."

Time to Find a New Creature to Be

shed skin snake smooth and new
to be envied like woolly bears crawling
over cool sandstone their lives built
around the necessity of constant
reinvention, I get fat instead
paint the walls gray, flap my arms
like a tiger moth, self-medicate
like larvae eating nitrogen rich leaves
like larvae playing possum
in the palms of children
in a pile of wool blankets
the coming ache of winter
restless incompletion

Solstice

June 2018

On the cusps of
balance and extremity,

say equinox without egg
then hold the sun in stillness

until hands burn Sonora.
On the solstice

glacial clocks glisten,
robins browd the gravel lot

their clock starts too—
How long before children,

before hatching before wretched
news dashes and are we waking?

Say solstice without son.
Say anemometer without

anemone, feeling the absence
of breeze, contrails still in the sky

that particular blue bubble
flecks of clouds—we are working:

Awdl cawl, a cist,
within our dim coracles—

Dream words unfluently
How long before children?

Papilio Ecclipses

You are out in the garden
though you are never out in the garden.

I catch you, black paint still wet
& cool against your fingers

One of our common yellow butterflies
adorned.

You call it a new species,
call this *An Enlightenment.*

You have given birth
to a counter-narrative

how we grow & how we know
a crisper process—

a laugh at Linnaeus.
One thing covers another.

We pin the poor specimen
to a board, to the wall
adorning

above the photo of your father
beside a small airplane

numbers & spots painted on wings.

II. FIELD WORK

Against Method

You are there in the lab working, solving. Repeating. Your lips shape waves into wonder. We want a medicine or a paint. You said we are trying to understand. You asked. Amidst the tedium of method. The comfortable lab coat of correctness. A drug. A cleaner. Rigorously executed failures. As planned. There is space between the acquisition of knowledge and wonder. One word fixes; the other opens. Space for a story. For accidents. Some grand phrase or trope like *the quest for knowledge.*

O, Mother of Chemistry. You sent me to play. Out of this clay and topsoil, these spring violets then dandelions. Out of pine sap and quartz, a wanting in me. I want to reproduce the glorious sugar maple, in graphite, a carbon allotrope pulled across a page that feels flat but not smooth. Full of the long fibers of trees. It has warmth and lacks perfection. I sketch the cattails and the millipedes. I hold the woolly bear. I let it crawl and cast its slow shadow over the sketchbook.

Resume

The job was to cut the grass, trim the hedges, pull the weeds.

It was to scrape the paint, then paint the paint.

I was to cover the naked paper with ink or graphite, words and images from nothing.

To place the washing machine on a dolly and lower it down the stairs.

I was paid for a week's training to go door to door as a census taker, but I was never sent out to take the census.

The job was to dip a plastic cup into the water over and over counting mosquito larvae before poisoning them.

I swept the halls and cleaned the courtyard.

The job was to write down carefully what she wanted to do with her life.

Some days, I had to ask the students why they drank in the dorm even though I knew why they drank in the dorm.

Hearing about sexual assault is difficult, but not the most difficult.

To clean up the trail of blood at 3am.

The job was to call for the 72-hour psychiatric hold.

It was to run the string trimmer along the outside of the penguin enclosure and the whale tank before the park opened.

I was discouraged from rhyming or using the word "soul."

Pull the sap buckets from the cold taps and dump them into the horse-drawn cart.

Chuck the hay bales in the wagon as it bounces over the ruts in the field.

"Hold this rope, and when I cut through the trunk of the tree, you have to pull hard in that direction, away from the house, then run."

The job was to read 100 collections of poems and decide which were the best.

That day we rode out to the wolf sanctuary and had our faces licked and wrote a story we never published.

Each morning I grabbed 3-6 homing pigeons and took them up into the canyon with me while I shot photos of whitewater rafters. The birds carried the images back.

I have to keep my lesson plan in my head when I go through the metal detector and walk past solitary confinement.

I have to catch the bird, the bat, the squirrel loose in the apartment building.

I rode my bike north of town at dawn to harvest vegetables and listen to people hum to themselves.

"You don't take off your clothes, and you don't get wet. 36 jets of warm water massage your body from head to toe."

I was not cut out for retail.

She is working on her English, putting her life into words and I just listen.

We were building trail high in the canyon and everywhere the beetle-kill trees were ripe for wildfire.

And other duties as assigned.

Empirialism

plantain tall in careless rental yards
                              tells us something

broad bitter in mouth leaves
ease pain as pulp over stings

bee sounds still
even as air cools to skin

stripping seeds from stem
feels like fingers over a zipper
                              tell me something
who was brave enough first
to put this medicine in their mouth

A Number of Inadequate Metaphors

She asks, "What do you mean by *responsibility*?"
Are we each our own dictionary? I wonder.
What I am trying to say—the opposite
of a heavy, infinite book we drag
through life until we can afford
a prominent oak stand in a prominent room
of our final house. It is also not lightness.

We write with people seeking refuge,
kids kept in prisons, in schools, in suffering —
I want to tell her what it is like to see their poems
beginning. I say each story is *contagious*, I say *viral*
— tired expressions. My words flow jagged,
some malfunction between signs, there's a chiral flaw
a failure of symmetry —

the words the woman translates for me, her story
I am trying not to tell, but to explain the feeling
of witness. My words miss her heat.
If I say it is a *gift*—wrapping paper
and Scotch tape, the world handed back to you
upside down or backwards, like reading in a mirror
new and surprising—not exactly. Not exactly
fireworks or morning dew, nor the miracle of air travel.

I could say, it is as if their stories lay on top of ones I know.
Like a simile, like a thaumatrope,
a wonder turner, and I have left the body behind.
These stories have scars and casualties —
On one side—hope; on the other—not hope,
not a thing with feathers on it.
There are hands twisting yellow strings;
you roll it between your thumb and index finger.
The string warms against your skin.

While I roll the details of another's life
back and forth, faster and forth, all at once.

And none of what is said conveys the girl's eyes
and breath, the feeling of falling
like when a word finds a word unexpectedly.

Glacial Legacy

for Edwin Andrew's Glacier

"I was here twenty years ago. It was more
than twice the size—a wall of ice," his body
melts into itself. He and I have spent
our breath to know our edges, our energies
that effort hollows—caves in, trips among talus
from middle French, of unknown origin.
A moment ago I was full of joy

for the vocabulary of glaciation
— Norse for *landslip*, for *glide,* the Latin *circus* —
and who names a glacier for a man?
The tarn is just above us.
Granite spires crumble in cloud
dragging over the continental divide.
The cirque before me, a man flowing
nimbly down the scree.

I clamber up, picking my way with my hands.
Sharp rock against skin shifting.
I had been feeling my youth.
I crawl into the cold bowl of stone,
wind funnels between Otis and Hallet's —
it is a force, a punch, a thief

sweeping breath from my mouth and lungs —
recreation and witness.
Who names a mountain after a man? And everything on it.
Obsolete, past-tense. I feel my pack tugging, the earth's core pulls
at my legs and chest. Muscles converse with gravity —
a body of possibilities on a body without.

Without Distance We Measure We

larger maps made of the smaller & smaller
this is not a time of geographical exploration

in laboratories light flickers, gives chase
certainly we are really not charting we

compasses, inappropriate in this traffic
sailing ships, not our escape from the cities

footpaths have all been mapped
follow the unimproved trail North

we ask and don't ask in our homes
give chase, if we are still we are not still

entirely like and unlike the high fishless lake
bacterial blue, cupped in granite

Don't Call It Pilgrimage
(We've Been Here the Whole Time)

I follow the interstate over the spine of the continent and find two Oklahomans from the Philippines on their way to Los Angeles. They do calisthenics in the snow beside their sleeper van. Sun sets fast behind thick clouds, the La Sals are shadow, and that's it: a few tents silent, windless, shallow fire breathes feeling into my toes. The tent asserts there is this space and that space: 'inside' and 'outside.'

— No, no pilgrimage isn't what I think it is. 'Inside' is shivering, a full bladder, it's leg-kicks for warmth in a sleeping bag. It's not sleep. This is a collapsable illusion, some warm air is trapped my breath condenses before turning to frost in the bitter hours. The state of matter between breath and ice is not a clear line.

I'm not a pilgrim because I did not leave anything behind. I just wanted snow-crunching under my boots and a raven begging at my camp stove. I wanted to blur the line between routine and life. The high desert altitude is the same as my apartment. The couple in the van takes twenty days to make a three-day drive. Now I have to think about the word *luxury*. I pretend to keep it simple: my pocketknife and loose thoughts, sandstone handholds, juniper berries in rust sand, an old book. A clockless flow of time shames ideas of 'to' and 'from' and transforms a word like transformation into something silly.

Over 33,000 Acres

for Valles Caldera National Preserve

canyons here carve through the expulsion of a great volcano
mesas are loose gravel and ash, your leg can posthole
as if trudging through deep snow, scents of juniper and sage

wind carries harsh dust and, though no thing is purple
the color pervades, then it is still, there are no people
only a surveying stick and very old pottery shards
rusted cans predating the "pack it in, pack it out" motto

then it is not still, the wind becomes fierce in the night,
the shadow of the caldera's rim looms and I am to be accurate,
and I am to avoid mimesis, and I am to bring the present moment
the pressing world into the poem

from all the things I leave outside these lines
the truth is I have no desire to drag this landscape
into the mess of our culture

the sound of a supersonic plane rends the quiet
but I am not fast enough to find the source
and it is still beautiful, it is still an escape
which is folding contexts into contexts

like geology and astronomy and postmodern warfare
the radio telescope angles, gazing at what and where
from its perch behind barbed wire and warnings of explosives

The Same Mixture of Fantasy and Avarice

—after Robert Smithson's Partially-Buried Woodshed

Pile earth on the roof of a woodshed
and when the center beam breaks
entropy and the National Guard set in.
An audible crack
breath hangs in cold air
the loader burns diesel.

Ground tumbles onto the roof
the sound is like drums
rolling down stairs
and satisfying
halt, hands steady on controls
the operator knows there is a vision.
Or a question with echo marks.

Campus is an infinite number of surfaces
a viscous liquid spilled on the hills
reveals how materials exists in time
how museums' acts of preservation
mask chaos and help us forget
futures. "What are we going to do about…"
presidents and how they say names of places—
Cambodia can be Lebanon, let's say Syria.

A one-ton bomb
crafts a crater when dropped
10,000 feet, it is aerial art. "A thing
is a hole in a thing it is not." What
kind of thing is a bullet?

Observations on Greatness

Of all the ways we might impress each other—
map and name the world after ourselves,
add places to some imaginary palmarès,
flex our syllable counts in classrooms—
my students narrow their eyes at this.

When we read *Frankenstein*
of course they side with the creature.

These dark dreams since the volcano,
since the crazed Italian scientist
reeking of formaldehyde and static,
since we began exploring the poles in earnest
in ships lit with the burning of whales,
since our mothers died.

I watch movie characters stitch up
their own wounds, bite the end of the string
take a splash of whiskey, flash a fleeting grimace.
I want to one up this for my students—
Sew a set of arms onto a slimmer torso,
shock a taller me into existence,
stroll into the room a self-made man,
a master of all the narratives of genius.

We ought to bury these dreams in ice
before they burn us
or we burn everyone with our wanting—
yellow-eyed and splitting at the seams.

I take great comfort as they squirm
underneath the horrible weight of greatness
a picture of men frozen in a lifeboat
or young Alexander von Humboldt
drawing a scalpel across his pale arm
vials and electrodes shimmering on the table—

A splash of antiseptic, the taking of careful notes.

Raise Your Arms and Make Noise

the park is empty
just the smells of ponderosa & elk musk
peaks ring the high meadow
I see—

fur flash / shoulder muscle ripple / feline tail swing

I can't hear anything over thick blood in my ears —

Make yourself big, I remember some saying
Don't run, or stare into their eyes.

The goal is to appear dangerous enough
to not be worth the calorie cost or injury risk.

This is easy for me,
I've spent my whole life pretending to be
more dangerous than I am
to avoid the hassle of masculinity.

Strength training improves memory
so I can easily recall
being dragged across the asphalt
punches landing haphazardly on shoulders
or with keen purpose on a jaw and the kicks —
playgrounds and bars
each hand on my body and the times
I fought back feeling my own capacity
to wound
until I was too strong
to be worth it.

I know what predators are capable of
words like a claw over a belly
I believe her description of
teeth clamped on the back of the skull
hot breath horror

this is where
the metaphor falls apart / or not
the lioness turns from the moraine filled with prey
to me, to the ridge high above
there are two possibilities—

     she is an ambush hunter &
     can stalk me from higher ground

     or she is afraid of man.

Against Method

the experiment fails
90% of the time, she says
and I feel that failure in her eyes
it clings to the white coat
lifeless on its hook
workers at the end of their solutions
in the middle of their shifts
empty of play and paradox
was hydra animal or plant
was it cloud or mountaintop
what if the all was permeable
the thickest, stablest categories
like *human*—what defines human
is a computer writing a poem
an elephant painting a landscape
a beaver changing its environment
prairie dogs barking a language
what can we say thus refined
that the experiment shows
one cannot resurrect their mother
in the university's O-Chem lab
or by leaching this student's wonder
we've got to put our own blood into this
like the mad scientists of literature

Outside Erfoud

there is a place in the desert
where a wave of black rock crests red sand
and in it an ocean—
coiled ammonites spear-like orthoceras
their soft bodies gone

our guide splashes some water on the outcrop
white ghosts

these dark waves that rise up needy
in our dry times
full of hunters
wanting

he ushers us into the shop
some stun, some imitate
we purchase a set of 4 polished coasters

years later
beneath the rings of our drinks
the Cretacous still haunts

when I set my coffee down to answer the text
a family of complexities
the defensive ink sack, tentacles scour
extinct jaws jealous of life
our soft bodies rile after each other

High Park

The wind has given up and uncanny
settles over us. Cyclists wear bird flu masks.
What is the wildfire like? They ask from the East.
I do not like the wildfire. Stars gone
mad orange haboob, the cutting edge of apocalypse.
A suspension, a cocktail, a dream—
this self-infliction whispers over June wildflowers.
Picture the waking streets of your hometown:
light scatters, filters, shadows gather substance,
the bright sky thick, everyday things like white
decorative shutters, brick and bark, more
terribly intense, worse the warm colors—
dull peripheries, a hefty vignette effect.

Baltimore

I keep thinking about this bird
in a huge exhibition hall of
a downtown convention center
the kind of room lit by a grid
ineffective counterfeit suns
the kind of room where you
could organize a half a dozen
soccer games or build
an elementary school
a room sunk below street level
with no windows, no breath
just plastic tables, black curtains
made from oil, burnt coffee
and the smell of sweat, cardboard
pizza on styrofoam plates, coke,
people labeled with lanyards
and this bird, small, earth tones
just a house sparrow adapting
her earthy feathers blending in
with acoustic tiles, each morning
she sweeps from perch to steel perch
long after I stop coming in
to set up our table display.
Is this what it is like to be a ghost?

Hay Cutting on the Western Reserve

There was an easy poem
about the workers in the field
repairing the red baler,
the hay on ground golden.

It would be written on a page
a few further on
than one that knew the names
of all the May flowers,
in which the forsythia
was forsythia and not a fissure
between your living soul
and someone on the other side
of death, every year the same
color.

And, by God, those workers
would be dignified, with grease
on their hands and the chaff of
alfalfa in their beards,

but the machinery
of culture has broken down
and we are our politics—
blind to each other, and it was
an easy poem anyway
that didn't know that rain
would ruin the second cutting.

About the River

In the 50th year since the last fire on the Cuyahoga

I've been talking to kids about the river
the way you talk to them about sex or drugs
or American history, by that I mean
in a classroom. The kids have been talking too.
One girl told me she went everywhere in a kayak
when her dad didn't have a car and I said
there's a long history of that. Usually they ask,
How can water catch on fire? I want to spin it
like a magic trick, like wine or rabbits; say
something French. But, I stick to a truth
and tell them that if they really want to
they can set the river on fire again. They
ask what will happen to the turtles if
the river catches on fire again. Ah, I say,
that is a very good question. And then,
we find words that rhyme with flood.
What, then, would the deer drink,
or anything with a mouth?

III. JOKES, LIES, HOAXES, MISTAKES

Aedicula Ridiculi

My mother opts for the encyclopedias to come all at once.
Then, each year, a matching addendum,
newly minted authority bound in cream,
pine green, gold accents, smooth paper,
glossed color images.
In the attic another set—*Britannicas*, 1912.
Onion paper, 8-point type. This reach,
a costly aspiration, expensive breath,
Yes, she says. An investment in us.

Subjects to this abundance.
At night perhaps just one letter, or just half of one letter.
A sliver of volume.
Bullfrogs sing in chorus around the pond.

Lightning bugs. Lingshan. Liege. Ligature. L did not have an entry for laughing while playing kickball on dusty infields nor S the spades cutting sod into shovel-wide squares. Holes the shapes of books. Filling with worms and childhood memories or the memories you want to give to others' children or the mud on your hands that you want to wipe down the smooth forearms of a friend ridiculously luminous all at once in the cool contact where you tell a fact about dreams about dredging machines about Dresden and they tell you theirs or you make new ones together an approximation of history for the new Sultans of Zanzibar you sternly walk towards the stern of the Dreadnought its great steel hull towering above the water. Fat shadows of 10-inch guns. Uniforms uncannily repeated. Then when it is safe together you make an entry into the altar of the god of laughter and joy in the Temple of Ridicule which stood on the authority of its stone foundation just outside the gate where Hannibal gave up his siege until we learned it was a typo in the encyclopedias.

Truthfully

I am as we are —
skin wrapped around
skeletons of mermen, misfits
made hopefully lovingly
27 bones in each hand
might have been relics
bits of buddhas and saints
you, the King of France
the book in your hand
fiction by fiction
a kind of magic mirror

the better part
of the world built on
lies might be cataloged
color-coated
there are six types of lie —
up, down, strange, charm
bottom, and top
hoaxes are antiparticles
to aggressive incuriosity
(a synonym for masculine /
antonym to safety)
we could talk about violent
sports or food alternatives
antithesis to business
as usual people exercise
create curiosities
ante up and
puzzle each other
this is and isn't
some degree of arrogance
some grave play

Jokes of Nature / Jokes of Knowledge

She and I look out over our backyard
choking on cottonwood fluff and possibility—

we want belief or we want to play
we might say, or make something
out of feathers, scales, and myths
at the edge of what we can know
that fills both the cup of possibility
and the cup of knowledge at once
pleases all nine little goddesses and
entertains neighborhood children
we can make anything:

egg-like magnolia-sized blossoms
        releasing soft, white mice from limbs
smelling of lavender and citrus
        fingers through fur

        feet feel the rumble
as a troika of 6 half-horse/half-fish noble beasts
        drags our chariot across the sands of Libya.
                        If not children
why not wings
        or a moon of Neptune, or the dark lightning of memory
why not the Giant of Cardiff and the Shroud of Turin?
Peasant farmers harvest the rich yield from the spaghetti trees
        in the early Swedish spring—
What's the difference between hoax
and jokes when in some languages the initial letters
        have the same pronunciation?
                Cover us in gold or
        marble.

The Man-Eating Tree of Madagascar

limbs snap fast, ropes of willow
whip bestial hunger
a fierce blend of exoticism
wraps, chokes the life out of
so many for half a century
thrashing in dark jungles
of white imagination
this kind of story a brother
might whisper to a sister
not all unlovingly

when we were children on our farm
helping to water horses and milk
the dairy goat, we would speak
against twilight words gathered
from fictions, gathered from
television—when the signal was
clear :: when the signal is clear
night smells of lilac
spoken words will gather weight
they become clouds the way
June became a cloud, the way Aunt
Ellen became a cloud, animate a
hollow suit of armor, vanish a black
cat, these powers belonged to letters

until reason bent words towards
ordinary, what had once been possible only
on impossibly long summer days was not at all,
instead syllables of chemicals, vocabulary
of phylogeny just different in jaw
from the repetition of spells
until spells became science
of cyanide in black cherry limbs,
death caps, sweetly scented, highly
poisonous maybells, ivy itch, clear signals,
chicory sleeplessness—I learn

some plants in the same family
as our philodendron can rob
our ability to speak: A man says

limbs stir underbrush
groan of wood
moisture, layers of blood
and it is so
until another person counters:
The facts are pretty clear by now.
Of course the man-eating tree
does not exist. Oh, what a spell.

White Nefertiti

for the Travel Channel

Giddy. They have used their computers
and artists' hands pressing clay, a knife blade speaking
eyelid, saying lip. And here she is—

[   ]

an African queen. White as paper.
She needs this paleness
the way the missing link needed
to have an East Sussex mailing address,

& the way the skeletons of mermen
must come from South Pacific archipelagos,

& how Ferdinando Cospi needed
Sebastiano and Angelica Biavati
to stand among his possessions breathing
beside the bust of Dante
and the monsters in his five-volume collection catalog.

He owned and owned a mirror which reproduces
a Pygmy from a Giant, a Giant from a Pygmy—
the most monstrous face from a beautiful one.

& an amateur archeologist poisons himself
with the chemicals he uses to craft his hoaxes.

They build up in the blood the way truth comes.

Scythian Lambs

We climb a green hill together
picking our way over stone fences
to the view of an island & shade of a tree
trunk splitting
under the weight of its fruit
each white pomme
a cotton-ball lamb
eyes mute with tenderness
kissed by the sun.

    //I would lie to you
    such a world of rectangle pupils
    and twisting horn
    such roots & soils
    such taxonomy.

        All would be possible again.

    We would spin wool
    fine as the rich white winter
    spun into a mangle of metaphor, dyed.
    I want to mend, unbend the tree
    & keep its fruit free from symbol
    fate of lambs,
    fate of apples.//

At the coast, gourds drop
from high cliffs onto water
they burst into birds.
& the world is full of geese
their harsh songs,
their commitment.

Knowledge pours from seeds
crushed between teeth
all your paintings are of pomegranates now
no use for zoophytes
they've been weeded to extinction.

The Dreadful Boojum of Nothingness

I see a maple grow through a beech
their slow dance gives me a word
that means to give something a mouth
and how does a tree find a mouth
find speech, in a partner, a mouth
and an ear, a pair, a twin, a gemel
it becomes hard to know which tree
is which, they are unnaming
themselves, like we are speaking
two languages of the same words
not your love language, you say
something that isn't ancient and poisonous
are we speaking, are we growing together
not you, beloved, and I, but all of us
a grove, say teaching without teeth
is the same as gardening without seeds
you say that everybody knows it
I drive again and again to the city
the sea and the desert, to see beautiful
things made by women and men
and then to the forest to unsee them
scared of our freedom
to not believe in things that are

Monstrous Symmetry

after Marcus du Sautoy

a man has 16 faces
      all at once
across four dimensions he
is what he makes and what

he lacks, he lacks symmetry
      and the will to still his reptile brain
      lacks a tie to compliment his mustard shirt
he has two lungs but misses something parallel
to the muscle of his heart

he is his wound
wound around
      his ghost

and he cannot stop himself
his child-self jumping in the sand
      his eager second-half self smoothing over
the awful thing he said smothering the memory of his lingering
eye

he's yellow teeth and swelling gut
is the kindest softness he ever offered
      to a stranger he is

a baby, a handsome photo
      a sunflower seed spiral of memories
shelled and held and giving and

it was the way he made me feel
endlessly

IV. EXPERIMENTS & TRICKS

Notice

"Follow directions. Be careful. A chemical laboratory at home can be dangerous, but it can also be fun."—Robert J. Brown

Morning train sounds
along the dark river
the still mill towers,
more of the houses
for sale now.

Town is a chemistry lab
what is added / what is taken away
how we react—do we hold each other
in suspension—combine
break down or combust?
One town all catalyst
new, spills over every day.
One inert. Others await results—

When the magnesium plant catches fire
it rains, reacts
brighter than the sun
uncontrollable
for days a light at night
through bare limbs
then our bedroom window
through walls of a factory
crumpled like newspaper
children dance in hard
freakish light
cast shadows of wild animals
on the walls.

Introduction

Cleaning out an old house, I find a red paperback, *333 Science Tricks and Experiments* by Robert J. Brown. The book smells like a book. Throughout its pages, wonderful and painfully literal step by step illustrations. Chapters organize activities by themes. "Sound & Other Vibrations" is where I would stick the poems. If they were really good they could go in Chapter 10, "Heat." If they fall short of their ambition perhaps "Projects to Build." Or, cheap in their use of resources, "Tricks." Some experiments deal with Psychology and others Magnetism. Each has three components succinctly labeled: "Needed." "Experiment." "Reason."

"Hear Through the Teeth" an experiment on page 11, shows a boy plucking a rubber band looped around some of his bottom teeth. Under "Reason," Brown explains why holding the band produces a different sensation from wrapping it around the teeth, "the soft flesh of the fingers reduces the sound when hands are used instead of teeth."

One night in Cincinnati a car slams into the outside of the apartment. Asleep, I heard it through the foundation, through the bricks, through the tuning fork of the metal stair railing, through my teeth like a big mortar on the 4th of July. How many celebrations reenact warfare? Flesh cannot match the vibrations. There is an experiment called "Explosions on the Kitchen Stove." It is instructions for making popcorn.

Mirror Tricks

Light goes in all directions
directly to your blue eye
to the mirror
indirectly to your blue eye
to the mirror and mirror
indirectly indirectly to your blue blue eye
the face is both the face
and the reflection of the face
the reflection's reflection of the face
incident impinges

incidents impinge
lay a piece of glass on black paper
shine your light, double the world
your world reflected in the child's blue eye
your world bent in her brown eyes
not a reproduction
a future, bent and diffused,
invisible lines crossed
invisible lines extending
into the invisible visible

How Far the Storm?

December 2019

The news is about storms on the horizon
except for the segment about weather

and a story about mass graves
in Tulsa being probed with radar.

That story is about an eternal storm
like Jupiter's red eye.

It is about shooting vibrations
into vibrating earth to find the hollows—

It's the kind of rain
that a white kid like me was sheltered from.

But we can see it now,
like we can see that lightning strike

in Philadelphia, in 1985, hit 61 homes,
fire fighters kept idle.

In '85 we were old enough but never told—
we can see it now. Sonia Sanchez

points at our 50 year-old wound, Kent State,
calls it the same, calls us brother and sister.

We can count the seconds between
explosions.

We can feel them in our teeth.
Even as one voice says

a storm is coming, another says it isn't.
When I was young I thought the rain fell

in such a generously democratic manner,
eyes closed and counting Mississippis.

#NerdAlert

I am sitting in my office with a rubber band in my mouth and the door wide open. Multifaceted delight in every bit of Brown's book for me. First, the reading, imagining, and doing. Then, ripping, erasing, drawing mustaches or pirate hats on the goofy faces. The critical part of me applauds his gender equal illustrations and faults their lack of racial diversity. His assumptions and vagaries give me every opportunity to work out a question.

In the instructions for building your own kaleidoscope: "Needed: A 5 x 7 dime store mirror, a way to cut it…" In other experiments we need three dead cells, a vice with plastic jaw inserts, a broom and three people, a lighted cigarette, sunlight, blackberry jam or jelly, an earphone from a transistor radio. Elsewhere, in an experiment titled "Can You Hold a Pencil" Brown writes, "Needed: A Pencil." In another, "Two fingers." Later, "A doorway."

I appropriate one experiment as his definition of poetry:

> *The teeth and jaws act somewhat as a sounding board, vibrating with the vibrations in the rubberband. The sound waves are conducted directly to the ears through the bones of the skull.*

I play with these words and make something that you might play with too. We might play together. Build projects. Make Heat. Feel Magnetism. Understand Biology and Psychology. Experiment with Sound. Dangerous tools, mild poisons.

Smoke from the Fingertips

with a little ammonia
we can rob your roses of red
turn hydrangeas
into ghosts of hydrangeas

you snap your fingers
a coil of white smoke
spells either wonder
or cheap trick or
we are out of matches now
aren't we

Ghost Light

It is a simple trick
a bare electric bulb in a dark room

even after you turn off the light
you still see it

not the cooled coil
in a simple cream-colored fixture

a full image
soaked into retinas

the idea is trite
when we think of capital-lettered deities

perhaps it is a richer metaphor
when we think of grief

of kids rubbing their eyes
in a dark room

of a young woman feeling
the sit bones on the bottom of her pelvis
rock right, then left
as she greets each thought and sets it aside
behind her breath
but she can still see their shapes
and the shaking in her chest
all around her lungs
is more than a flutter, much more
for a long time, none of us understood
that the work we do on our spirits
isn't a lonely work

Tricks

In one experiment Brown simply requires "Observation." In another, he wrecks the inquiry in the same line where he issues the challenge:

> **Experiment:** *Try to find two leaves exactly alike. It is impossible.*

As a variation of one trick, intended to mock the mind's misjudgment, its misinforming of muscles, he begins:

> *If there is access to a chemical lab, find a container of mercury and ask someone to hand it to you.*

That's the whole joke. He expects the unsuspecting chemical lab attending adult to misread the weight of a container of mercury. Heavier than they thought. In print, it's stupid. The naked, serifed letters. The overwrought *gotcha* in the Reason. And, it is absolutely the kind of thing I would do were I regularly in a chemical lab with a jar of mercury sitting on a shelf nearby. I'm also going to find two leaves that are exactly alike. There are roughly three trillion trees on earth. Each year we cut down ten billion more than we plant and I'm closing in on halfway through my life, if I'm lucky.

In his introduction, Brown claims possession of "three erudite and meticulous consultants who check everything." This is the kind of help I will need.

A Note on the Text

Brown's book wasn't mine,
not my house.

I was helping
another family.

The book
payment in a pile

& an intersection of
ambition and abandon.

Marred with graffiti
an object imbued—

— with nothing of my mother.
But I thought I might

children and science
become one or another

father and mother
all that chemistry
the whole slew of
human experimentation.

Almost enough
for every day of the year.

About the Author

I begin to get a sense of Robert J. Brown's house in 1984. There is a shelf stacked with dime store mirrors, an old Folger's can full of dead batteries, piles of scrap wood, counterweights from old windows. He has a small cabinet of metal sliding drawers full of string, wire, wax paper, cheesecloth, ball bearings. Little bins: carefully labeled for screws, bolts, nuts, washers. Doubled with metric enthusiasm. There is a glass mustard jar with old nails in it.

His wife, Mary, says the projects are supposed to stay in the garage, but the chemicals are carefully organized in a cabinet in the basement. Not locked and not out of reach. Based on the illustrations, his family has the same silverware we had. He keeps a jar of mercury just for a laugh.

Perhaps I knew his son Robert J. Brown, Jr. or his daughter Betty, the book's dedicatees. Patient Mary is known for her lemon bars. She is among the kindest examples of her generation. I don't pity her casual sufferings. Robert makes dinner on Fridays where he flirts with grease fires just to show RJ and Betty how to extinguish them with baking soda. "See Betty, See Mary, there's no need to panic!"

I don't think he's vain enough to call his son Junior, but I can't be sure.

Capillarity

salt water / soapy water
rubbing alcohol / oil

the phenomenon is about how we absorb
differently

alcoholism / heartbreak
my wordward bend cooling

the phenomenon is about resilience
about orientation

to difference
sex / love /decency

her hot temper
& body betraying

strips of paper towel
cotton balls

salt water / pills dissolving
the countertop forested with glasses

family / family
the control group is siblings

in absence
nature / nature

how we absorb
& resist

what goes in
& out

until the fibers of paper
can hold no more

Don't work alone. Have someone with you, ready to turn off a switch if the experiment goes wrong—and this can happen with the best of us.

— *Robert J. Brown*

After experiments end
instructions run out

I make coffee
before you wake

we sweep broken glass
out of the car, glitter of dawn light,

write new directions
as fast as we can read them

both kinds of work
frantically.

Switches everywhere
for the lights, for train tracks

the memory of analog tape
roll back the audio,

words in our mouths
add inertia, anchor us to our current

other words derail, disrupt, dream
bring us close to needing.

Place our curiosity
on display

or in a fireproof cabinet.

Notes

In Vivo. My mother's lab produced a number of chemicals for medical applications. One worked 'in vivo', or in the living organism, and reacted one way to living tissue and another to dead tissue.

Beast Machines. Parts of this poem are indebted to Lisel Mueller's "How I Would Paint" and also to the Dutch and Flemish painters on display at the Cleveland Museum of Art.

Weekly Weather Report. From Li-Young Lee's "Words for Worry."

Glue A Paper Globe. Susanna Crum prints maps and globes, cyanotypes, woodcuts, lithographs, that ask questions about our relationships to places.

Time to Find a New Creature to Be. The title comes from a line in the song "Not Kansas" by The National written by Matt Berninger.

Papilio Ecclipses. In 1702 William Charlton, an English butterfly collector, painted spots on a common Brimstone butterfly and sent it to Carl Linneaus claiming it was a new species. His hoax lasted for decades.

The Same Mixture of Fantasy and Avarice. The earth artist Robert Smithson created "The Partially-Buried Woodshed" on the campus of Kent State University in the months before the May 4th, 1970 shooting. Sometime later, the date was painted on a beam of the collapsing structure. The quote in the final stanza is a Carl Andre motto which Smithson titled a 1968 essay after. The title of the poem comes from W.H. Auden's *Enchafed Flood*.

Jokes, Lies, Hoaxes, Mistakes. These poems draw from many sources, including *The Museum of Hoaxes*, which "explores deception, mischief, and misinformation" including a section on "Lusus Naturae," or Jokes of Nature. References to Marchese Ferdinando Cospi's cabinet of curiosities which included living humans, Edmund Spenser's Man-Eating Tree of Madagascar, and zoophytes that confuse the categories of plant and animal.

Aedicula Ridiculi. Caroline Wazer, of Atlas Obscura, writes that a latin typo misnamed a tomb on the field of Rediculus the Temple of Ridicule. The story surrounding it described a temple erected to mock Hannibal's failed siege of

Rome. While false, it was treated as fact for more than a century.

Jokes of Nature / Jokes of Knowledge. The title comes from Paula Findlen's research on 16th and 17th century scientific jokes.

The Man-Eating Tree of Madagascar. In 1874, Edmund Spenser fabricated and published an account by a non-existent German explorer, Karl Leche, of a man-eating tree in the wilderness of Madagascar.

White Nefertiti. In February 2018, the Travel Channel unveiled a 3D recreation of Nefertiti on the *Today Show*. The resulting sculpture appeared to many to be startlingly light-skinned. The Piltdown Man, presented in 1912 by Charles Dawson, claimed to be the missing link in human evolution and asserted all our roots to be British.

Scythian Lambs. The Scythian Lamb, or the Vegetable Lamb of Tartary, is a zoophyte, or a plant that resembles or becomes an animal.

The Dreadful Boojum of Nothingness. "the Dreadful Boojum of Nothingness" is a phrase of W. H. Auden from *The Enchafed Flood*.

Monstrous Symmetry. Du Sautoy's book *Symmetry* explores its title concept from mathematical perspectives. Du Sautoy researched a symmetrical form, referred to as "the Monster:" a great, symmetrical snowflake which exists in 196,883-dimensional space.

How Far the Storm? While the title is one of Brown's experiments, the poem draws heavily from a visit by Sonia Sanchez. Sanchez visited Kent State in the fall of 2019 as part of the commemoration of the 50 years since the May 4th shooting. She urged us to look carefully at other events and to look up the 1985 police bombing in Philadelphia.

Charles Malone grew up in rural Northeastern Ohio, headed west to the Rockies, came back to the Great Lakes, and has loved all of it. His chapbook *Questions About Circulation* is out with Driftwood Press as part of the Adrift Chapbook Series. He edited the collection *A Poetic Inventory of Rocky Mountain National Park* with Wolverine Farm Publishing. Charles now works at the Wick Poetry Center at Kent State University coordinating community outreach programs.